# Our Own Westside Love Story

# Our Own Westside Love Story

## WITH WORDS FROM TONY TO MARIE
## INCLUDING POEMS BORN OF ENDURING LOVE

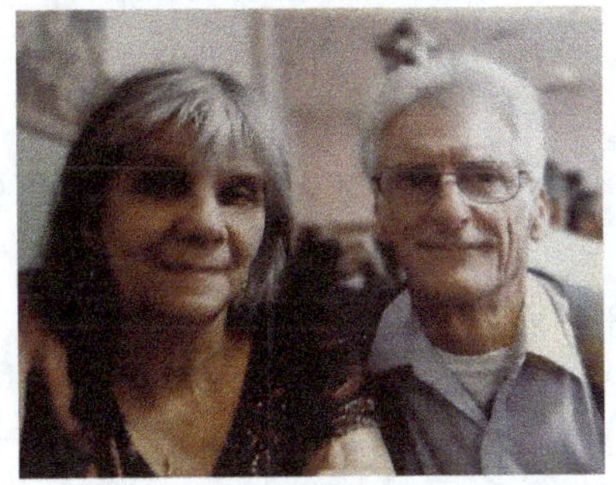

Anthony R Balista

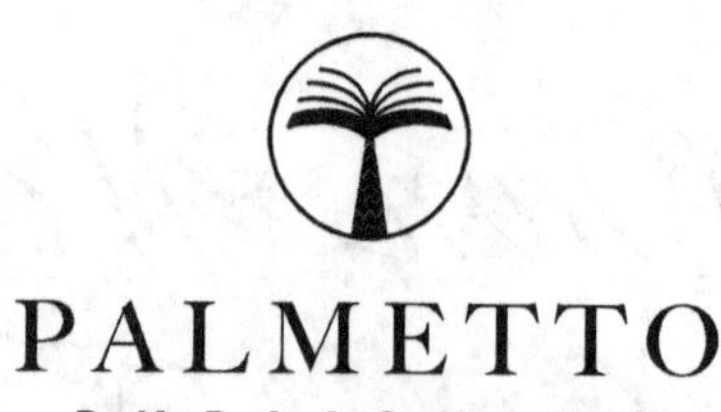

# PALMETTO
## PUBLISHING
Charleston, SC
www.PalmettoPublishing.com



Hardcover ISBN: 979-8-8229-5008-5
Paperback ISBN: 979-8-8229-5009-2
eBook ISBN: 979-8-8229-5010-8

# ABOUT THIS BOOK

This is the story about two people, Tony and Marie, whose paths in life had actually crossed many times, so close as to be in the same place, but never in each other's view. They were both alone, living their lives mundanely but with the purpose of trying to succeed in their own singular endeavors.

Both had endured broken hearts from betrayal, having tried their best to make their relationships work. And as the song goes, by Gene Pitney, "only love can break a heart and only love can mend it again".

Both had accepted their fates, and as lonely lost souls in God's vast universe were simply going on with their lives, hoping someday that they would find some modicum of success, totally unaware of God's plans. But then one day God decided it was time for them to cross paths once more, and to mend their hearts.

This is their love story, and the words of love Tony felt for Marie over the years, as narrated by him. One thing is different. This is not a movie or a play!

DEDICATED TO:

*Marie Martini Balista,*
*My Eternal Soulmate*

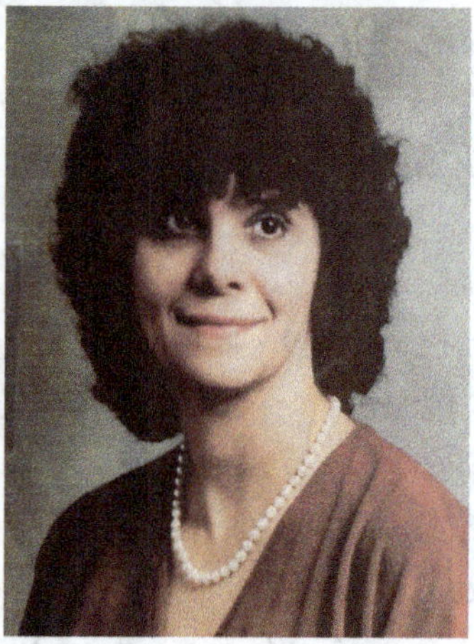

TO ALL WHO LOVE:

*Harken to these words of love, for they are born of lessons learned from an angel who was my soulmate, lover, and friend of 33 years, my darling wife, Marie. She now rests in God's loving arms.*

*She was, and is, and ever will be the epitome of all good things God could have ever put into one living, breathing, human soul. Our love shall endure through eternity.*

*Anthony R Balista*

# CONTENTS

## *OUR STORY*



## WORDS OF LOVE

-*1*-

# THE BEGINNING

*I had just returned from Europe, having completed my sixth Army overseas deployment and had taken an extended leave. I had accrued so much leave that I needed to take it or lose it. I was three years divorced. I was on the last leg of my leave and had finally arrived at my home town. in Warren, Ohio. I had almost enough military time in to retire and had decided to check out the job market in my area, having been gone for almost 23 years.*

*It was Monday and only five days remained before I had to sign in to my new duty station over 500 miles away in New Jersy. So, I went to the one job placement agency that had been doing business in town for over fifty years and would know, if anyone would, about the local job market. As I walked in the door, I was greeted by Marie. I explained my situation and she agreed to take some time to look at my current resume and talk about the job market in the area.*

The owner who was out sick, would have normally done it. Considering my circumstances, she agreed to fill in. Marie was personable, professional, and beautiful beyond words. I had never seen her before in my life. Had the owner not been sick I probably never would have met her.

We talked at length about my goals, the local job market, my resume, and job opportunities. As we closed out the interview, I asked her if she would have dinner with me as I was bored after 54 days of leave and would be departing in five days but would enjoy some company. She accepted and we scheduled dinner for Thursday, the evening prior to my departure.

Other than confirming our date Wednesday in a short conversation, I did not speak to her until our date. Thursday came and I picked her up and we went to dinner and then decided spontaneously to take in a movie since the evening was young. She was conversant, personable, charming, and beautiful. During the movie, as we laughed at a scene, I felt compelled to hold her hand. As I reached for her hand, she unhesitatingly but gently placed hers in mine. You could have picked me up off the floor. In an instant out of nowhere, I felt literally dizzy, euphoric, and overwhelmed by every pleasant feeling that a human could experience in a lifetime. It was actually scary and I was speechless.

In reality, it took a while to refocus on the movie. She seemed oblivious to my reaction but never let go of my hand for the duration of the movie. And I suddenly realized God himself was telling me she was no ordinary human soul. She was my destiny. Yes, in one meeting, it hit me that hard.

As we walked to the car never letting go of each other's hand, we made small talk about the movie. As I drove her home my heart and mind desperately raced as I pondered what to do and say, knowing that if I said nothing and moving over 500 miles away, I would probably never see her again. I couldn't shake the strange overwhelming feeling that gripped at my being. I had never felt like this before and just couldn't understand what was happening. I was so overwhelmed. As I walked her to her front door and unlocked it for her, I knew I could not leave her there alone. To the day I die, I cannot explain what came over me. So began our Westside Story.

Without thinking or hesitation I gently took her in my arms, and calmly said to her these actual words, "Just where have you been hiding all my life?" I want you. You are everything I will ever need, and I need you to be mine for always. I can't leave without knowing you will. I can't explain it, I just feel it".

She did not shirk, or back away but simply put her arms around me, looked deeply into my eyes, smiled at me, and gently said", Oh I've been here waiting for you and if you want me, I am yours" And we sealed our promises, then and there with a kiss. I didn't want to leave, but really had no choice since I was facing a 500 mile drive in the morning. I departed, after assuring her I would return the next weekend. I went right to bed but couldn't sleep. All I could do while lying there, was see her face and feel her lips on mine. I finally drifted off knowing in my heart she was sincere and that she was mine from that minute on. After all my emptiness and loneliness, God had completely filled the void in my soul in an instant.

Before leaving in the morning, I stopped at the local florist, and bought her 2 dozen yellow roses to be delivered at her office because she had told me they were her favorite. I knew then and there I could never live without her and told her so again in the note I wrote and had delivered with the flowers. I drove 1000 miles every weekend to be with her until we were married 5 weeks later. She had a special aura about her and a distinct delicious scent that never left my tastebuds in all the 33 years we were together. I could actually taste her any time I touched her. She was delicious.

# -2-

## OUR FIRST WEDDING DISAPPOINTMENT

Getting married was somewhat complicated since my divorce and hers were in different venues and since I had been out of state for so long. However, we finally got our marriage license but faced a major hurtle. We could not get married in the Catholic church since her ex-husband even though he had deserted her, and left her destitute after cheating on her with five women, was alive, an absolute insane chauvinistic rule. But I loved her beyond all things and told her we would get married even if an Eskimo had to do it.

So, we went to a small community church in town to be married by the pastor. We wrote our own wedding vowels and the pastor was gracious enough to let us use them. One of the most important things that we said to each other on that glorious day was that our love for each other was for "eternity" We refused to use "Till death do us part" We meant it then and even though she has been with God for ten years, we mean it now and always.

*We had no maid of honor, and no best man. Only her mom, her dad, my stepdad, and his girlfriend, the pastor and an organist, and us. We always reflected on our special day and would laugh every time, we attended a lavish wedding of a friend or relative, because we knew we had the best wedding one could have. After her ex died a few years later and we already had our son, we received dispensation and married in the Catholic church. We had a small wedding with several guests, a maid of honor, and a small reception, but it never could hold a candle to the first one. We always cherished our first time more.*

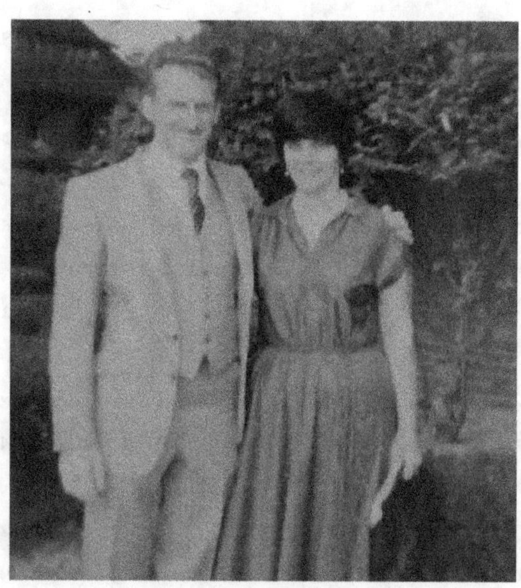

*OUR WEDDING DAY*

$$-3-$$

# A TOUGH BEGINNING

Over the weekends that I came back to spend with Marie, and every day in the evening when we would talk by phone, we told each other about our pasts, our previous marriages and all the things that had occurred in our relationships. We did not hold back. My ex told me as she walked out the door that I was right in my suspicions, that she had married me just to get away from her parents and out of their house. This was after 15 years of marriage and three children.

The only problem was that I had known it after six weeks of marriage. Marie's ex told her she was worthless and he was leaving after approximately 8 years of constant cheating on her with five different women and using the mortgage money for his girlfriends and letting her find out after he left her that their house was in foreclosure. He was supposedly taking care of the mortgage payments she would give him, even though she was the only one working. She lost the house as she struggled to survive and had rented a very small, one bedroom house in

Warren. She struggled to pay the rent and if it wasn't for an understanding friend of the family who owned it, she probably would have been on the street.

I knew all this because she told me, but then a few more things happened. And I felt so bad for my darling Marie. Three weekends after we were married, as we were planning her move to New Jersey, the phone rang. I answered it and a voice asked if this was Tony. I replied "Yes." The voice said, "this is Bob and we need to settle up on your jewelry bill." I responded, "what Jewelry bill? I believe you have the wrong Tony. I'm Marie's new husband."

Bob quickly apologized and said he was sorry. I told him, it was no problem at all but to tell me about the bill. After hearing the word "bill", Marie's face now carried, a look of horror. It seems that her ex had been buying jewelry for all of his girlfriends and telling Bob that it was for Marie. And Bob, being a close friend of Marie's father had been letting it slide. However, it was beginning to add up to a considerable amount, and her phone number was the only one Bob had for ex Tony, so he had called seeking to get paid.

I told him I would be down to talk to him. Marie was crying and embarrassed but I told her not to worry as it obviously was not her fault, but I would talk to Bob so her father would not be upset with Marie. I paid the bill off with the agreement that Bob would not ever let Marie's father know about it. He agreed. I loved Marie and did not want Marie to ever be embarrassed. Her father was a very strict old fashioned patriarchal Italian from the Old Country who would have taken it out on Marie. He ruled the roost and sometimes would not even let his wife speak. Being Sicilian-Italian myself, I understood completely.

But since I was an Army officer, I was easily accepted by Perry Sr. (her father) and her mother Angie, since Perry's older son was a career officer, and a Naval Academy graduate. His son, Perry Jr. and I hit it off fabulously and were close friends from day one till the day Marie died and have remained so. We coincidently had the same birthday and would joke about the fact that we had that day in common with one of the worst human beings that ever existed on the planet earth, who was also a military officer, - Adolph Hitler.

Two weeks later, Marie and I were able to move her to my military duty station at Ft. Monmouth, NJ. It had taken a few weeks for me to acquire Government Quarters. Then fate struck again. Poor Marie! This time I think she thought I would walk out on her. About three weeks after we had moved, I was returning to quarters from duty when I observed a tow truck hooking up Marie's car to be towed away.

I immediately confronted the tow truck driver and demanded to know what was going on. He informed me that her car was being repossessed. I immediately informed him., in a not so polite manner, that the car wasn't going anywhere and that he had approximately 10 seconds to unhook the car before he would be arrested. This was a military installation and he had no authority to be on it for that purpose. And I would have him arrested in a heartbeat. Marie came running out crying and hysterical.

I demanded the phone number of the lienholder from the driver and immediately called them. I told them that under no circumstances were they going to tow the car, and asked them how much was past due. They told me. I also asked what the payoff was. After they gave me the figure I countered and told them their court costs for an attorney to collect would exceed my counter offer because they would have to have to come back with an official court judgement. They agreed and we settled for my counter offer. I told them I would write a check on the spot and give it to the truck driver. They agreed. I wrote the check and he left.

Marie was hysterical, and crying, and so very upset. I took her inside and calmly took her in my arms and told her that nothing in the world mattered more than the love I had for her. And that if there was anything else I needed to know about, just tell me now because I loved her and was there for her and that I did not care about her past, or anything else, just loving her. I held her in my arms, kissed her, and calmed her down. She had been struggling for a few years since he had left her. And she thought that her troubles would never end. That was the last time we got surprised. I think that was the moment when she realized that I loved her unconditionally.

*4*

# A SMALL WORLD

Over the years we discovered our paths had crossed many times in inexplicable ways to the point of almost being in the same room but never seeing each other's face. Here are some notable ones. One day Marie told me about working previously in a plastics factory in Champion., Ohio. Apparently, one day the shipping manager, "Angelo" came in to the production office where Marie worked as the production scheduler.

He told her that he had just made a job offer to a soldier who was working for some extra money while on military leave from Vietnam. He had been so impressed that he told the soldier he had a job any time he wanted it no matter when he got out of the Army. He said the soldier had taken it upon himself, since there had been a lull in orders for the last week, rather than to sit around, to clean up and consolidate the whole shipping department on his own without any prompting.

At the time she told me about it, I started to laugh hysterically. When she asked me what was so funny, she gasped when I told her that soldier had been me. We never saw each other be-cause the shipping department and the production office were in different parts of the factory.

In high school she and her girlfriends would hang out at the local Dairy Queen, less than two blocks from her house and her father's barber shop. I would go there all the time between caddy jobs at the country club. We both knew the little old lady who would always give me extra ice cream in my vanilla milk-shakes because I was respectful to her and she had taken a liking to me. But I was always there at a different time and never saw her.

I never saw the inside of that barbershop until her father gave me a pre wedding haircut after we met. He cut hair for over 50 years for everyone who was anyone in that town and was known and respected by everyone. He actually came out of the Navy as a shipboard barber. He was a proud, hard-working man

The most shocking moment of realization came the time we had been married approximately one year and had been in-vited to a wedding reception in Ravenna, Ohio. The parents of the groom were "best friends" with Marie's parents and had known them for decades. Marie was excited to go and I was ex-cited for her. She told me about them on the drive to Ravenna. All my family and relatives were from a nearby town called Kent.

The reception was at a large hall in Ravenna. It was ex-tremely crowded with a couple of hundred people. As you en-tered the side door, there were people sitting in a long hallway on both sides facing each other engaged in prolific and an-imated conversation. As we entered the door my jaw dropped down to the floor for there on the left were a dozen or so of "my aunts, uncles, and cousins vigorously engaged, laughing, and joking, with Maries' aunts, uncles, and cousins, on the right side of the aisle.

As we walked through the door, there was immediate stunned shock and gasp as we recognized each other. It just so happened that my family were also mutual "best friends" of the groom's family and they all knew each other. What a glorious surprise. It took Marie and I a week to get over it. We had always been that close to each other and never knew it. We were overjoyed and realized that God had brought us together. We knew from that moment on it had been our destiny to love each other.

## -5-

# OUR GIFT

Ater about an additional year of duty, I decided to retire from the Army. Marie and I decided I would take a civilian job for us to be near my three children from my first marriage. I had turned down an offer to relocate as IT Director for the World Bank because Marie and I were concerned for the welfare of the children and we decided to stay in the area. I could not refute her logic because of the love and devotion she had shown them in the short time she had known them and I could see that she loved them unconditionally.

One day shortly after purchasing our home in Clementon, NJ, Marie approached me in a quiet but serious mood. She explained how much she wanted to be the mother a child of "ours" that would represent the love we had for each other. She explained that her ex-husband had always told her she was not worth having a child with and would be a terrible mother. She also explained that she understood the obligation I bore by already providing for my other three since my ex-wife had custody and I was paying child support and alimony for them and we were buying a new home.

She told me she would always love me and respect me regardless, if my decision was to not want the additional responsibility. I knew she was sincere and I loved her even more for her sincerity, honesty, and willingness to share her heart's inner thoughts and insecurity. I turned to her and looked into those loving eyes of hers and told her that no woman on this earth could ever be a better mother than she had already been to my other three, and for the unconditional love she had shown them. I told her that I was honored to be chosen as a father to any child she would bear. I then laughed and jokingly told her that if we were going to get her pregnant, we had better start practicing right now!

Marie was so excited, but unfortunately, we lost our first child due to miscarriage. Back then, any woman age 40 was considered high risk and the doctors were somewhat paranoid about what a woman should or should not do, their diet, activity, and many other factors. Marie was so desperate to be a mother that she became depressed after losing our first child, and almost gave up because she felt that it wouldn't be possible to bear another. I had difficulty convincing her that we should keep trying because she had been so devastated by her loss.

Six months later Marie woke up with the "flu" and a fever and not feeling well. That flu and fever turned out to be an 8lb, 10oz. boy we named Anthony Jr. She was ecstatic as I watched her hold him on her tummy as he came into this world. She was in heaven and I was too. I have never seen a woman love a child so much as she loved him. But she always gave love equally to all four and they loved her as their own mother.

*-6-*

# DON'T EVER SAY:
# "I LOVE YOU TOO!"

From our first night together, Marie and I realized that our love was mystical, real, enduring, and beyond what most people could ever understand. It took just one night and our lives were transformed forever. Just to hold her hand gave me an incomprehensible warmth and glow that was unrelenting. It never went away and there was always a palpable sensation that overcame me in her presence or while touching her.

In the beginning of our relationship, as we intimately shared our pasts, our pains, our betrayals of the heart in consummate detail, we realized that our feelings for each other ran far beyond the normal human level of sensitivity. We both looked at our feelings for each other as "sacred". We vowed at the onset that there was one phrase of endearment banned from our vocabulary and never to be expressed to the other, should one of us say to the other, "I love you." And those words were spoken to each other several times daily.

As strange as it may seem, the phase we both vehemently loathed was: "I love you too!" After what we had experienced in previous relationships, we felt that the term "I love you too!" was something that could be easily said without feeling or empathy to simply placate the other party as a copout into believing they were cared about. If you think about it, it is much harder to initiate the words, "I love you", which is an initial expression that has to come from actual feelings from within the heart, and a desire to express them to the one you love.

"I love you too" in our way of thinking was just a knee jerk response that was much easier to placate or cover up feelings with. We had been through it a thousand time, knowing in our hearts, it was only a cover up from that other person. To us, this was nonnegotiable. And from the second week of our relationship until the day God took her 33 years later, we never once "EVER" uttered that phrase to each other. That was something we could actually feel disdain for and took as serious as our vows of love. We could not stomach a verbal disagreement and avoided them like the plague. No one I know on this earth could ever say they watched or heard us raise our voice to each other.

We could not envision our love being temporal or till death do us part. Whenever we had a serious discussion about our love for each other, which occurred quite often over the years, we would be sitting in our chairs talking about everyday things. Suddenly, she or I would look across at each other and stop talking. I would then take my hands and slap them on my knees and motion for her to come to me.

It was a private solemn ritual never performed with anyone else present. And silence would suddenly fill the room. Marie knew it was time to come sit on my lap. We would always open the discussion, with me saying, "You know, I love you forever!"

And she would reply, "Yes, I know. I love you! forever" Then I would put my head on her chest and listen to the beating of her heart. I loved to hear the beating of her heart. It was nothing for us to sit there for an hour and just relish our closeness. It was always glorious.

It was nothing for us to cling physically to each other for hours after love making basking in the glorious touch of each other and feeling an indescribable glow of unspeakable joy. No one ever understood how close we really were and how much the word "soulmate" was apropos to our mutual existence.

We could sit at a place like "Dunkin Donuts" and be enmeshed in each other's presence to the point of oblivion to our surroundings or others who had walked through the door, recognized us, and would then be trying to interact with us in conversation.

We had a standing humorous response to those who could somehow manage to get our attention, but were unfamiliar with our deep connection or interaction. Typically, we would receive a very intense almost concerned inquiry as to why we were "so into each other that we seemed to be unaware of other people's presence in a public setting, and just how could we be so in-love?" Typically, it would come from the waitress, or even another patron couple at a table adjacent to us. This predictably occurred as I would be holding and kissing Marie's hand. Of course, not being teenagers and having our wedding bands be clearly visible, it was always the same question.

We found it fascinating as we came to believe that apparently older people over forty just weren't supposed to be that "in-love". Marie would play the innocent unaware mortal that suddenly would apologize about our deep conversation and inattention to our surroundings and wait with a straight face for our punchline that I would provide with serious demeanor as I would struggle to keep from laughing.

I would typically respond with a serious look and, "Oh, sorry we're not married, just dating, and we decided to try it out for the first one hundred years and then if works out, take the plunge." You have no idea of the incredulous looks that we would receive, especially if it were a young female waitress. Then we would burst into laughter and watch the look on their faces as they realized they were hoodwinked.

And then we would tell them about our chance meeting and our one and only date, and our sincere love for each other. They would always walk away with a look of amazement. There are so many people in this world dying to be loved. We had it all and never needed more. No one ever could have loved or received more love than we from each other.

# -7-

# OUR STRUGGLES

Having been successful in the military, and earning my commission up through the ranks, I found out that "civilian life was a lot more hectic in some ways. Upon moving to NJ, Marie initially took a position with a NJ based recruiting firm near the base and when I retired from the Army, she actually placed me in my first position with RCA Corporation as a senior systems engineer working on the Navy's Trident Submarine.

Having an extensive electronics and IT background across the spectrum as an IBM certified customer engineer, programmer analyst, and with operations management background, I was able to lead the successful completion of a major communication systems specification in excess of one thousand pages, for the Trident Submarine that was 3 upgrade levels behind and 3yrs past due. This put me in good stead and I was soon recruited from RCA to head a Hundred Million Dollar development program for another company called "Aydin Computer Systems", located in Horsham, PA that was building "Over the Horizon" Radar system displays for the Department of Defense.

Things were starting to look up. And Marie was doing well as a recruiter. And we were so much in love. We had not yet had Anthony so our lives were filled with each other. This was the one time in our lives that we actually were able to enjoy some together time. It didn't last long enough as life got more complicated.

Company politics were starting to rear their ugly head. And I soon realized that doing your job the right way in the civilian world was not always the most popular choice or easy. There seemed to be a moral courage conflict with honesty and ethics at times sometimes being scoffed at. It took politics if you wanted to get ahead faster. However, my principles were not for sale and Marie told me that no matter what the outcome, I should stick by them. And I always loved her for that.

When I was first hired at Aydin, I had been told by the VP of Operations that I had been hired to get to the bottom of the problem concerning the organization's inability to get our prototype system into the production phase since we were still in prototype phase. A year and a half later, including six months of research into program budget reviews, scheduling issues, and engineering development meetings, trips to our Client (General Electric) and other issues, I felt I had come up with an answer.

When I told the VP and Program director my perceived picture of the problem and showed him our perceived shortcomings, I was basically told that they had made a mistake in hiring me since he obviously had to cover his tracks. As an executive level manager, I was given sixty days-notice because I refused to fudge the numbers and hide reports that unfortunately disclosed the problems we faced and reflected his lack of planning and leadership. I was never one to hide the truth.

The CEO advised me to hang in there and that a full-scale program review would be taking place prior to my departure and that since I was still Program Manager, I should prepare my presentation. This resulted in a three-day heated closed door program review with the top brass, including the CEO, all VPs, department heads, and the Director of Programs (my direct report), plus external consultants. I went prepared as always and had a plethora of supporting documentation regarding my findings. That program would have been worth billions in today's dollars.

However, you just don't go into a meeting of that significance with nothing more than a ball point pen and a song and dance. We had a Hundred-Million-dollar contract at stake representing at that time 65% of the corporation's total revenue stream and the potential of cancellation at the end of the fiscal year at stake, due to our failure to deliver. Unfortunately, both my boss and the VP of Operations were competent politicians but not competent engineers, planners, or managers.

After two and a half days of intense scrutiny and program review, the CEO suddenly stopped the meeting in the middle of my presentation. I had been disclosing the serious problem areas of the program I had uncovered as well as proposing solutions to the group. And everything I said was constantly rebuffed by the VP of Operations or the Director of Programs in front of everyone. It's always a tough battle when you're the new guy on the block. After all, he had his ball point pen and a piece of scrap paper to write on versus my 6 months of intense involvement and tons of documented findings.

At that point, the CEO's words would not have been fit for publication. Needless to say, the CEO chopped off a lot of heads on the spot including demoting the VP of Operations in front of everyone, and flat outright told the Director of Programs to "censored" pack his bags right then and there. This had been an organization where team players were not welcomed. It seemed that it was every man for himself - a direct converse of what I had learned about teamwork and cohesiveness in my military career.

Marie knew that first day as I left for the meeting that I might be let go, but told me that I should not worry, and just do what was right. She always supported me. In our 33 years of togetherness, she never once criticized my principles. She always showered me with love, support, and devotion in my greatest successes and during my most dismal failures. Boy was I ever happy to call her afterwards.

As he terminated the meeting, the President demanded my immediate presence in his office. I figured it was the end of the line. He then told me that I had saved the program and the company 8 million dollars and that all of my proposed solutions would be implemented. And that my new much fancier office was just down the hall. And that from now on, I had open door access to him any time. But I knew that by doing my job right, I had made a lot of enemies. I was taken off that program and put in charge of an even larger one where my direct report was now a different Vice President who gave me support, respected my decisions and listened to my inputs. But the handwriting was on the wall. When I went home and told Marie what had occurred, she told me it was time to go start looking for other involvement.

I took her advice and let myself be recruited to ITT Corporation as Deputy Engineering Manager for a much larger 200-million-dollar Air Force program where I was brought in at a Senior level over incumbents due to the delinquent nature of the program and the infighting of the primary contractor, Hughes Aircraft Corporation and Subcontractor ITT Corporation (US).

On my way out the door to ITT, I informed my boss the VP and the CEO at Aydin that they would lose the new program I had been assigned to within a year because the company culture of "survival of the fittest politician" would catch up to them. It didn't even take that long before I got the call from the VP that my prediction had come true.

ITT was a much larger corporation and I quickly discovered that the culture there was just as politically driven if not more, than what I had left behind. As I advanced up the chain of responsibility over the years, it became ever more apparent to me that teamwork was not the norm. It didn't take long to realize that this program was in even more dire straits that the one I had left. After only four months of nightmare revelations, and observations, I stuck my neck out and had the nerve to tell the Vice President of Operations of a 500Million dollar corporation that he was going to lose his program.

He was livid to say the least, and his response not printable, and when I told Marie about our interaction, she jokingly asked "if I would have a job in the morning.? "To be truthful I wasn't sure after that meeting. Due to my observations about the status of what I perceived to be a critical situation, I had gone about ten levels over my bosses' head and he was madder than hell.

But Marie stuck by me and said that it was better to stick to my guns than to get involved in the politics. Marie always had my back and had faith in me. She knew how principled I was and that was one of the reasons she loved me so much. Principles cost me much in my life but Marie's love for me made it all worth-while. I had always been candid in the military environment and refused to get involved in the bureaucracy or back stabbing politics.

This was a tough job and the 210-mile, daily drive to work and back at ITT made for a 5am to 6pm day. The Vice President of Operations was also a seasoned politician and walked with eyes in the back of his head to keep from getting stabbed in the back. A month later I was abruptly called into his office and figured that my new job of 5 months was being terminated. I called Marie and told her I thought, once again, this was it. She told me to keep the faith and not to worry as we would be ok. Much to my surprise the VP asked me just how the hell did I ever know that this 200 million dollar program would be cancelled as I had only been there 5 months. I told him the truth. I figured I was fired anyway.

I let him have the sarcastic truth. The truth was that the 160 engineers and 10 department managers that reported to me were too busy infighting with each other than doing their jobs or honoring schedules. And that since I was the one who monitored the financials for the program, money was constantly being wasted and that the Prime contract Program Manager and the Sub contract Program Manager, instead of working together, were too busy arguing over who had the best-looking necktie for the day. We were also overrun to the tune of 40 million dollars.

He was astounded and I was shocked when he told me that due to my intuitiveness and straight forward approach, I would no longer be working for the engineering department but would now report directly to him as his internal investigative corporate troubleshooting consultant, a much kinder term for the role of hatchet man. Over the next two years, I pointed out both major problems and proposed solutions to them. No one liked it when I walked into their department if I heard of a problem.

He once told me that I was the best technical engineer he had ever met but a lousy politician to which I whole heartedly agreed. And within another year he sacrificed me to the political God's for his own gain. I left by mutual agreement. His career ended abruptly a year later with death from a massive heart attack from the stress of internal corporate politics. Someone I had become close friends with in the company called me and informed me of his passing.

*-8-*

# DOWNHILL FROM THERE

At this juncture we decided that after ten years in the corporate world, unless we owned our own company, the corporate world was not for us. As bad as it got, Marie and I had our love and she never gave up on me even though it seemed we were losing every material thing we had.

But my darling Marie stuck by me through it all. I managed to acquire an occasional consulting gig but was unable to land another full-time job in the tech industry. Things got progressively worse and we lost our home and everything we had struggled for. At the time we purchased our home, because of state regulations, the seller was not required to disclose the fact that our home was located within the red zone (1/2 mile) of one of the ten most toxic landfills in the United States.

Since we could no longer keep up with the mortgage, we were forced into bankruptcy. Since the state law had changed in the 10 years we owned the home, we were forced to disclose the existence of the landfill. We could not sell the house at all and ended up with a ton of negative equity and all the thousands we had invested in our home was lost and we were forced into foreclosure. This was one of the most discouraging moments of our lives.

And though we cried when we had to leave all our hard work behind, we never stopped loving and it just brought us closer together. We then decided since the children were now getting out on their own, and Marie's father's health was beginning to fail, that we would return to Ohio and watch over her father. Her mother was handicapped and used a walker so was basically unable to care for her husband other than cooking. He still had his barbershop but was subject to bouts of illness which made it difficult.

I tried to open a small home repair business but because we had so little resources for tools and equipment, I was forced to work out of my car. I built a small wooden trailer to pull behind the car but it was inadequate for many jobs. The one upbeat thing was that our youngest son was a positive distraction for Marie's parents and he was now around 6 years old.

Marie decided to start her own recruiting business and with the investment help from a close family friend, since we had no money or credit, she was able to open her own office. Within three months of opening the office, Marie was involved in an almost fatal car crash having been rear-ended by a small snowplow. I was then forced to stop what I was doing and jump back into the corporate stream to help her since she was physically partially disabled and suffered back and nerve injury. Again, we faced potential disaster. There wasn't enough money for both of us to take a paycheck so I never took one. The business struggled for seven years and due to most of the industry in the 50mile radius of our business comprising steel, rubber, and small manufacturing, going belly up, we lost most of our potential clients and were forced to take a loss.

We also lost her dad who had become seriously bedridden, and requiring constant care with numerous emergencies taking us away from business at critical times and occurring frequently. Nevertheless, family came first. Marie was the consummate combination of Mother Teresa and Florence Nightengale combined, and the epitome of compassion. Her father's well-being far exceeded the concern for a profit. I loved her more than words can say because of that.

When we lost him, part of her went with him and it took until her mother became ill, that she was able to overcome the grief that she carried in losing him, by focusing on her mother's needs. Some times when we went (regularly) to the cemetery to pay him a visit, I would hold her in my arms until she regained her composure. Marie was a special loving creature who cherished her father.

*-9-*

# PICKING OURSELVES BACK UP

To get us by I obtained a business loan from a local small business redevelopment consortium to expand the home repair business to a serious level. Marie's experience in recruitment and interpersonal phone skills were a Godsend. We handled every type of small (one-man) repair you could imagine. I also had a special category of repairs called "one of a kind" where I would fix anything that you wanted repaired that no one else would touch regardless of age or item.

This turned out to be a successful venture and we obtained "BEST OF THE BEST" Handyman repair award from our local newspaper for three consecutive years running. The newspaper ran an annual public survey and a list of approximately 50 categories you could vote for. We proudly ran the business for a combined total of 22 years without a single registered complaint and even though not registered with the BBB, received countless referrals from them when I would ask the customer who referred them.

Two years prior to Marie's death, I retired the business. In the interim during the five of our business years Marie's mother and brother had passed on and we were finally done with 19 solid years of caretaking. Marie's mother was a sweetheart and we took care of her at home so she felt secure. Her care was complex and demanding but I had promised Marie that we would never institutionalize her no matter how bad it got. After the years of devotion Marie gave me, it was the least I could do for her.

Marie was an angel and had also given the same intimate level of care to three other women. A church parishioner, a semi-homeless woman we both knew, and her very good friend who was a die-hard alcoholic.

These were all people to whom she gave hospice level care at times. I am proud to speak of her intense and uncompromising compassion and goodness to humankind and supported her in every way I could. She never once complained, always put herself last, and gave me love, devotion, affection, and loyalty, in abundance beyond any man's wildest dreams.

To this day, I don't know how she did it and sometimes I truly believe she may have been an actual Angel that decided she wanted to see what it was like to live amongst mankind. So, God let her try it and see what it was like, and then told her it was time to come home.

-*10*-

# BEGINNING OF THE END

*It was in September and we had just buried my own mother who was estranged from me for most of my life. As a child of eight, she had been raped by her own father and never recovered from it. And being a male of the species, she never let me forget it. It was a long sad story but my siblings and I buried her next to her first husband, my blood father whom I had tragically lost at age ten.*

*About two days later I awoke from a horrific dream and experienced a foreboding omen. I saw my love Marie lying in a coffin surrounded by grieving relatives who were sobbing hysterically. It really got to me but made sense considering what I had been observing for a while. For the last six months or so, during our evening walk, Marie seemed to be losing her energy, and the walks became labored and shorter to the point that sometimes she would beg off completely.*

*I hadn't given it much thought, but suddenly with the omen, I became concerned. I told her she needed to get a checkup* and had written her an impassioned letter about my love for her and my concerns for her health. She had assured me that she was fine even though I could see the difference in her demeanor, daily activity, and lack of energy.

Just before Christmas, it happened. As I picked her up from the church office where she worked, a couple of the staff expressed their concerns to me about her shortness of breath and what they had observed that day. She assured me she would be fine and we stopped for coffee at Dunkin where we did often. She seemed better but suggested we pick up a decongestant.

We did and she took one when we got home. An hour later, she complained of difficulty breathing and we immediately went to the Hospital Emergency Room at St. Joes across the street from our home. I literally interrupted the emergency staff as she complained she could not breath. She immediately lost consciousness and was medevac'd to St. Elizabeth Medical Center in Youngstown, Ohio. She would have died if it hadn't been for an extremely alert and skilled nurse who intubated her immediately with a respirator.

By the time I got to St. Elizebeth they had confirmed congestive heart failure and excessive water on her lungs. The next day as she regained consciousness, she was informed of the heart failure. And family cardiologist told her the of the urgent need for quadruple bypass heart surgery and was told she would not survive much longer without it. We were stunned and overwhelmed.

She went in for surgery in March of 2014 and although the surgery was successful, God took her into His Loving Arms 49 days later as a result of total organ failure and Sepsis due to an incompetent ICU physician and staff. I practically lived there for that period of time. Less than 48 hours after her surgery, another Dr. who claimed to be an associate of the heart surgeon informed us that during surgery when harvesting veins for her bypass they had discovered that her left leg had no circulation and it would require additional bypass surgery to save her leg from gangrene and amputation. Only 48 hours after massive heart surgery, she endured yet another massive bypass surgery on her leg.

Upon completion of the second surgery, the surgeon bragged of his successful venture and I was assured that things were fine. He never showed his face or checked on her leg again but sent a snobbish non communicative associate to do the follow-ups. I finally cornered the associate and let it be known in no uncertain terms that I expected communication since I was her caretaker. The only communication I ever received of consequence is when ten days later they advised us that he had to amputate her whole leg. Yet in all things, Marie never once complained.

The end came at three in the morning of the 49th day when I was called in only to be told that if she were kept on the three blood pressure medications that she was receiving, that her body would literally burst in two and that she would not be able to endure further medication and that there was nothing else to be done. She was already swollen to the point of being literally twice her size.

I had no choice but to make a heart-rending decision to stop the medications. I held her hand, prayed to God and watched the beautiful heart that I has listened joyfully to for all those years stop beating. I sang her our song, kissed her goodbye, and reluctantly released her into God's loving arms. I was devastated.

The funeral was delayed for a week due to the atrocious swelling and stretching she had endured from the medications which disfigured her beyond recognition. But I knew that she would not want to be confined and so proudly stood beside her opened casket as I greeted the bearers of condolence. She had this little soft cloth non-descript doll only four inches tall that she would hold and cuddle at times she didn't feel well or was under the weather. We called him: "Lovie"

Just before they closed the casket, I had my talk with "Lovie". He told me he would take good care of her so I tucked him into her arms and kissed him and her goodbye. I knew she was in good hands With GOD and "Lovie". At the funeral, I gave the Eulogy and proudly thanked my love for all the tenderness, compassion, love, generosity, forgiveness, and goodness she had shown me over our 33 years together and for being the best thing that ever had happened to me. I laid her to rest knowing she waits for me. It was by far, the hardest thing I ever had to do in my life.

## -11-

# THE MIRACULOUS VISIT

The first few weeks alone were devastating and I could not find a balance or solace. I cried myself to sleep at night clutching her picture that I would hold to my heart. I had emptied a bedroom completely of any and all items that would cause me to think of Marie and would go there periodically so that I could close my eyes, and clear my head and momentarily stop grieving. It wouldn't last long but it did help. Sometimes I had to go back three or four times a day. It was my way of coping. We all cope or grieve in our own way.

About two weeks after her burial, on a particularly harsh day of tears I went into the room, sat down next to the dresser, and closed my eyes as I usually did. I just sat there trying to defuse my grief. I wasn't crying but I felt an unusually strong level of sorrow that day. I sat there in dead silence with eyes closed trying to fend off my exceptionally heavy despondency.

When suddenly, I felt a wisp of a breeze brush my face. It did not startle me but simply caused me to open my eyes. To my utter shock and astonishment, there appeared on the dresser in front of me, a beautiful floral card, the type that you would write a note or greeting into. To this day I cannot tell you where it came from for the room had been empty when I entered. There was no envelope, just the card standing up

There was nothing on the front but the flowers. But inside were these shocking words: As I read the words, I burst into tears and sobbed hysterically for half an hour nonstop, clinging to the card and holding it to my heart until my throat was raw. It simply said, "I love you", and was signed "Marie" in her unmistakable hand.

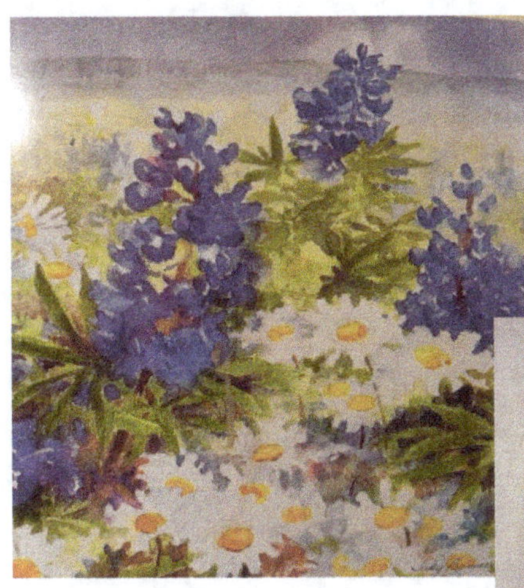

THE CARD

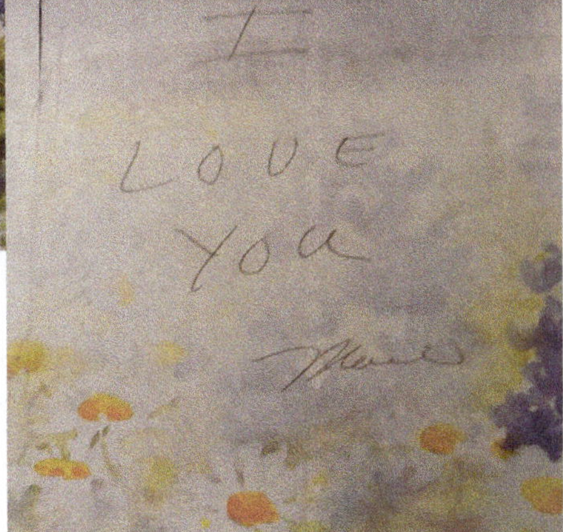

For those of you who believe in miracles, that was mine because from that day on, I knew Marie had made it home and was safe in God's loving arms. Either God had let her deliver it to me or the angels brought it for her. I cannot tell you which way it was.

It really doesn't matter. I can only tell you that it actually happened and I know she loved me beyond life itself and was concerned enough for me to ask God to help me manage my grief. But after I finished crying that time, I never needed to use that room again. So that's our story.

# EPILOGUE

As of the writing of this story, it has been ten long lonely years since God took her home. But each and every week since her passing, yes each and every week, I take several bouquets of fresh cut flowers to her grave as a testament of our love for each other. A lot of flowers over the years, but a ton of love.

And always, when possible, they include one bouquet of yellow roses. I will do so until the day comes when God allows me to take them to her one more time and hand them to her. Our love for each other is eternal. After all, when you are talking about eternity, it was only yesterday when she left and I will see her soon.

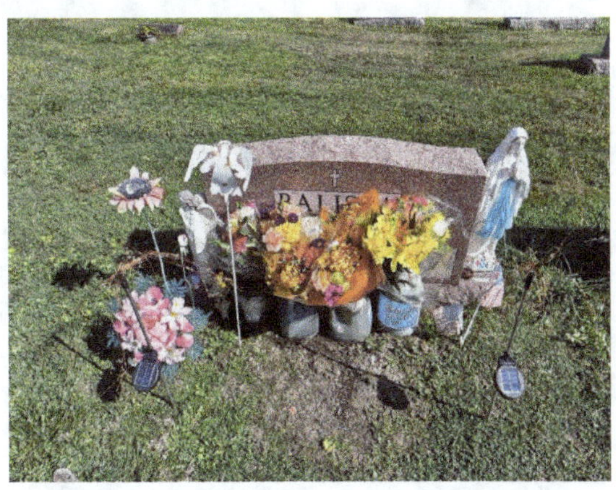

HER AND MY RESTING PLACE

Of the words I have written to honor my love for her, some are new and some are very old and are words that I wrote to her years ago. But regardless of when I wrote them, they all reflect the love I carry for her in my heart. She taught me what love was all about. So, I share a few of the many hundreds with you and anyone who needs to feel love like we feel.

Rest well my darling Marie, for soon we'll be together again and we will sing our song of love thru eternity!

All my love, Tony

Words Of Love
To Marie
Thru The Years

# MY OWN WORDS

*Regardless of fate's cruel joke on me*
*Putting me where I never chose to be*
*I am faultless and innocent as are thee*
*But it changes not what God lets me see*

*I have no guilt for what I feel*
*Or words I write for they are real*
*Nor apologize for what I know*
*Fate has put beyond my control*

*I have no need of words to copy*
*I use no words with which games to play*
*For when one means words from the heart*
*I must say what I must say*

*Therefore, search for all you will*
*To find the words from another's pen*
*Waste not your time looking in vain*
*Because the words come from my heart within*

*MY WORDS TO YOU ARE FROM MY HEART*

# A LIVING SOUL TO LOVE

I looked at you a while ago
You made me look when I saw in your soul
Warmth and beauty

You captured my heart and lifted me
You healed my spirit and set it free
With your tenderness

If I could have you in my life
To love and stand by thru all strife
Paradise would be mine

Loving you is everything
Loving you makes me a king
With riches beyond compare

So, turn me not away from you
I will love you till my life is through
For I have found heaven

I have not a choice
You have captured my heart
There is no escape for my soul

THERE IS NO WAY TO STOP LOVING YOU

# BE NOT AFRAID TO LOVE

When we look for the love, we want for our heart
When we long for life's dream of happiness found
Sometimes we get bruised and we stumble about
Not knowing what under the rocks may come out


Sometimes we are cut and are scraped and are torn
Sometimes we feel heartache and sometimes feel scorn
But we continue the search with the hope we won't fail
To find the "kindred heart" which is our holy grail


But if we stop looking under those rocks out of fear
Or turn from the search when the chance is so near
What we search for may never become crystal clear
And we miss for the chance of that love to appear


I'VE NEVER BEEN AFRAID TO LOVE
AND I AM NOT AFRAID OF LOVING YOU

# A LOVE LIKE NO OTHER!

I want our love to be

A love like no other love

Warm and tender and sweet

A love that poets would acclaim!


A love that has no end

A love that penetrates the walls

Of our souls and ties us

As one to eternity


A shelter beyond the stormy seas of life

A love to hold us up beyond the reach of time

That fills our every want and need

As we are one indeed!


I WANT TO LOVE YOU LIKE NO ONE EVER HAS OR WILL

# A BASKET OF LOVE

There was once a princess lovely and fair
With flowing locks of golden hair
She was tender as the starlit night
And warm and gentle her heart shown bright

Her father the King and a goodly man
Said, "it's time for a suitor to seek your hand"
What do you desire they offer you
Let's find suitors for you to woo!

They came from all over the kingdom
And many came from a foreign land
But no matter the things they offered her
She felt no compulsion to give one her hand

The King thru frustration had heard and seen all
For the princess refused to heed anyone's call
She said to her father, there is nothing I feel
Their offers of kingdoms and castles seems nil

My heart feels no comfort in castles of stone
For in Castles of Stone, my heart still feels alone
So the king decreed that whomever could give
This princess his daughter a reason to live

Would indeed win her hand contrary to norm
Be he prince or be pauper if he could perform
The magical task of giving her reason
To live happily with him through each of life's seasons

Many more came but she always said "NO"
The king watched them come smiling and frown as they'd go
It all seemed so hopeless as she'd rejected them all
Only one suitor left standing quiet and tall

He stood quiet and strong and spoke not a word
His clothing was simple and almost absurd
His eyes gazed upon her and looked not away
She was mesmerized, quiet, didn't know what to say

For unlike the others, he rushed not to speak,
For the others seemed desperate, or nervous, or weak
She studied him curiously and with stinging word
Asked, "what do you offer I haven't already heard?"

He smiled at her simply and held his hand out
A small basked covered with flowers and woven from reed
And said, I have looked in your heart, it has spoken to me
And this basket contains all you will ever need

It holds love and devotion and tenderness too
Compassion, forgiveness, and love that is true
A lifetime of caring till death do us part
Faithfulness, passion, and all of my heart

So, I offer this basket in exchange for your hand
Loving your heart always and I pledge to stand
Always with, behind, and beside you too
Till the angels take us and our life is through

So, search not for gold or castles of stone
But for love and tenderness and to not be alone
For God sends his goodness from up above
In a small basket, a basket of love

YOU WILL ALWAYS BE MY PRINCESS EVEN IF I'M A PAUPER

# MY TREASURE IS YOU

Though gates of gold he will never see
Nor diamonds, pearls or rubies rare
Man wastes his fleeting time on earth
In search of treasures rich and fair

The oceans' bottoms, the caves, the beach
Always slightly beyond his reach
And yet he continues, searches anew
For the end of the rainbow's golden hew

He struggles with weariness, anger and pain
Battling with obstacles threatening his gain
Always one more impediment pushing him back
Trying to defeat him and throw him off track

No end to the turmoil that pulls on his mind
Causing him question if the treasure he'll find
Doubt starts to haunt him and burden's his soul
And make his mind wonder if he'll reach his goal

I scoff at him, laughing, at his wasted time
For he seeks petty trinkets in comparison to mine
My search is over, my quest is through
I have found my treasure for I have found you

YOU ARE THE TREASURE IN MY SOUL

# DON'T BE CRUEL

Don't be cruel to my heart that loves you
Love is so rare and fleeting these days
Don't be cruel to the heart that loves you
For my heart loves you in so many ways

Don't be cruel to my heart that loves you
Don't take my greatest joy from me
For loving you is all I live for
No greater love there could ever be.

IF YOU COULD ONLY FEEL WHAT MY HEART FEELS FOR YOU

# HOW LONG I WILL LOVE YOU

In the silence of the night, I lay in your arms and you in mine
No words pass between us, our voices silent, unneeded, and respectful
Of the music of the universe, that plays out before us
Its magnificent display of breath-taking beauty abounds as the
Shooting stars light up the night sky before our very eyes.

We are speechless and overwhelmed by the display of beauty that
Flashes before us and it humbles our senses and our souls
I cling to you ever closer and you to me as we feel the glory of our
Love permeate our beings with the rhapsody of joy and peace.

We have no wants, no needs, no fears, no desperation for we
Are one, in mind, and body and spirit, and our love flows through
Each other like a whispering brook that refreshes, and cleanses
And gives sustenance to our souls.

You will forever be my love, my everything, my eternal soulmate
And eternity is but a moment in time compared to
how long I will love you.

I WILL LOVE YOU BEYOND THE END OF TIME!

# LOVING YOUR HEART

You were not yourself today.
I could sense some deep emptiness,
And a quiet pain that sent shivers thru me
As I sensed your sadness and despair rumbling
Louder than the rolling thunder.

Your sadness was palpable
Your aching heart's message visible in your tears
And your sense of hopelessness ringing out
Louder than the church bells of Saint Mary's.

"BUT KNOW THIS"

In the darkest day of your life
When all seems hopeless and
Every hope that you could imagine in your mind
Has seemingly abandoned you
And even God seems out of reach.
Know even then my dearest

"YOUR HEART WILL BE LOVED BY ME"

# BE MY SOULMATE

Come to me with your tender arms
Enfold me with their embrace
Let me feel your warmth within me
Be tender to this fragile soul
Who longs for you

Take away the frustration of the day
By melting into me with your tender love
Let me feel your lips on mine
And move with me as one

Let me taste of your sweetness
And soft tender love and feel
The ecstasy of your touch
And be buried within its bliss

Let my soul bond with yours
Let the glorious radiance of our togetherness
Refresh us and give us peace
Knowing that our souls are as one

THESE WORDS SPEAK FOR THEMSELVES

# I HAVE NO CAPE

I have no cape with which to fly
I cannot carry you to the moon
I cannot walk upon the clouds
For me there is no silver spoon

But in my heart is love for you
Measured not in earthly things
For loving you gives me so much more
Than all the wealth of the richest king

For all the things you are to me
Beauty, tenderness, so much more
Splendor beyond my wildest dreams
Loving you makes my heart soar

LOVING YOU IS MY HEAVEN ON EARTH

# WE HAVE FOUND PEACE

As the night wind blows gently across your face and scatters
Your hair across your forehead, fluttering its' strands into swirls
The glow of the night stars competes for dominance over moonlight
The crickets' song rings out in harmony with the hooting of the night owl

They blend together in a rhapsody that rings sweetly in our ears
The melodious sound calms the spirit and lifts our hearts
And we float along the river of calmness and delight
Buoyed by the knowledge that we share in our hearts

The softness of your touch and warmth soothes and comforts my soul
For I am in my heaven and my beating heart sings a song of joy
There is nothing more that I could wish for
Other than to want your loving embrace to last thru eternity

And though the ecstasy of you is real and touches my soul
I feel the weight of reality as it is gently but irrefutably set before my eyes
For my eyes see that life is fleeting and our presence is temporal
For some day death might take you away from me and out of my reach

The thought infiltrates and disrupts the joy of the moment
And generates an anxiety that could feed a growing despair
But my heart knows the truth and I swat it away from my mind
Because our hearts and souls have made other plans

That we will be true to each other and though our flesh becomes dust
We will love each other thru eternity and our love abounds forever
For we have found our peace and have overcome our fears knowing
God himself has heard our vowels and blessed our promises to each other

OUR LOVE IS ETERNAL

# PLEASE TELL ME

Tell me please what I must say
Or do or be or which songs to play
That would lift you up and make your heart sing
And fill your soul with the best of everything

What's good and warm and makes you know
I would walk through the storm and the winter's snow
To touch your heart and warm your soul
And give you all of my heart.

THERE IS NOTHING I WOULDN'T DO FOR YOU, MY LOVE

# SOME THINGS NEVER CHANGE

If I could live a hundred years
Beyond where I am now
Some things would remain steadfast
No one would dare ask how

It would not matter the path I'd go
Thru arid desert or winter's snow
To the pot of gold at rainbow's end
Or the starlit sky where horizons bend

The path could lead thru the depths of hell
Or thru heaven's gate where the angels dwell
To the shining sea or the ocean's shore
I'd find them no matter where I'd pulled my oar

For there are things that can never transform
They're eternal and magnificent throughout life's storm
Things God has made undeniably true
The tenderness, beauty, and splendor of you

YOUR HEART AND SOUL WILL ALWAYS BE BEAUTIFUL TO ME

# WHAT SHALL I SING

What words will make your soul to sing?
What inspires it to make it soar?
What touch can give it ecstasy?
To know the joys of love and more!

How can my heart touch yours?
To make you feel love's embrace
To lift you up in all things glorious
To win the prize of this life's race

Speak to me and tell me true
What lies withing the heart of you
That brings such joy within my being
And joins my soul with yours to sing

WHEN I LOOK INTO YOURS EYES MY HEART SINGS

# THE DAILY JOYS YOU BRING TO ME

I know you wonder why you are to me
So much more that words can say
You claim innocence to having captured my heart
And filling my life in every way


At sunrise your smile awakens me
As I feel the warmth of its radiance
And gives my beating heart strength
Strength to face life's hardest dance


Midday brings me other joys that flow from your loving glance
I touch your hand and feel your loving embrace
Knowing all is well within my heart
You've granted me the courage to run life's daily race


And as the evening shadows grow longer from the setting sun
I feel the peace and the warmth of you soothe me
As the essence of your soul intertwines with mine
And we become one

BEING WITH YOU GIVES ME EVERYTHING I NEED

# THE ECSTASY OF YOU

My heart lives to hear the song that your heart sings to me
The joy, the sweetness of the song fills my heart with ecstasy
I feel the touch, the tenderness, the warmth of your embrace
The joy that swells within me causes my beating heart to race

I draw you close into my arms to taste the warmth of you
The tender beating of your heart my hope it does renew
There are no words that can describe the depth of the joy I feel
There is no doubt that within my heart, the joy you bring is real

You are my dream, my hope, my prayer, my aching heart's delight
You bring to my heart a rhapsody lying in my arms tonight
If I could live a thousand years and feel this joy you bring to me
I would beg God for a thousand more to never end my ecstasy

YOU TOUCH THE VERY DEPTHS OF MY SOUL

# THE HAUNTING WIND

Listen to the wind as it whispers through the trees

Does its' melody sooth your heart and give you peace?

Does it sing a song to your soul?


Or does it's echo ring in your ears and awaken

In you the memories of the pain once felt by betrayal

Of your love and the helplessness of being tossed away like a stone


As your heart and soul withered from the blackness of despair

And the hopelessness and emptiness overwhelmed your reason

And you felt lost beyond hope


Come, let me lift you up above the storms of sadness

OLet me fill your soul with sweet tenderness that heals

And give you the loving from my heart

That will caress away the ache and once again make you whole


Do not tarry for time steals all things from us

And turns good dreams into history that cannot be rewritten

The time to be loved is now for tomorrow may never come


LET MY LOVE FOR YOU HEAL YOUR HEART

FOR ONLY LOVING YOU CAN HEAL MINE

# TO LOVE YOU

*There is no toil I would not endure*
*There is no place I would not be*
*There is no mountain I would not climb*
*To love you tenderly*

*There is no path I would not walk*
*There is no sea I would not sail*
*There is no desert I would not cross*
*My love for you shall never fail*

*So, tell me the price that I must pay*
*Open my eyes that I might see*
*What I must do to prove my love*
*And have you give your heart to me*

*PLEASE GIVE YOUR HEART TO ME*

# FOR THE GLORY OF LOVE

For the glory of love

I will live my dream

To hold you dear in high esteem


For the glory of love

I will hold you dear

And within my heart forever near


For the glory of love

You will be my song

To be sung with joy the whole day long


For the glory of love

I will cherish you

Beyond all things for my love is true


For the glory of love

I will give my all

For you my love I will not fall


For the glory of love


PLEASE DO NOT DENY ME THE GLORY OF LOVING YOU

# ODE TO MARIE

I sit here and deep within my being I feel the emptiness
A void unfathomable, so deep as to be terrifying
It clutches at my very soul, and pulls upon my spirit
Eliciting pain and sorrow beyond description

For this morn as I awoke turning over in my bed to hold You tenderly
and seek the solace of your arms
The raw truth struck out at me with a blow of agony
That shook the foundation of my very being

And in an instant the actuality of your physical absence
Caused me to gasp and crushed my aching heart, as the awareness
That you were no longer here in our bed
Struck me a brutal blow, for God had taken you home

Shock and emptiness reverberated once again in my chest
As tears welled up inside me knowing that this recurring
Remembrance of loss and emptiness would unsparingly
Repeat itself again and again.

You were my life, my love, my very existence all wrapped up
Into one glorious being of beauty, warmth, and softness
For you were and are the epitome of everything good that God could
put into one living, breathing, human soul.

And though I ache with unbearable and overwhelming
Despair, and it seems that nothing is worth living for,
Know my love that I live on for you, loving you beyond
Time and space until God reunites our souls.

WAIT FOR ME, FOR I LOVE YOU BEYOND THE END OF TIME

# ABOUT THE AUTHOR

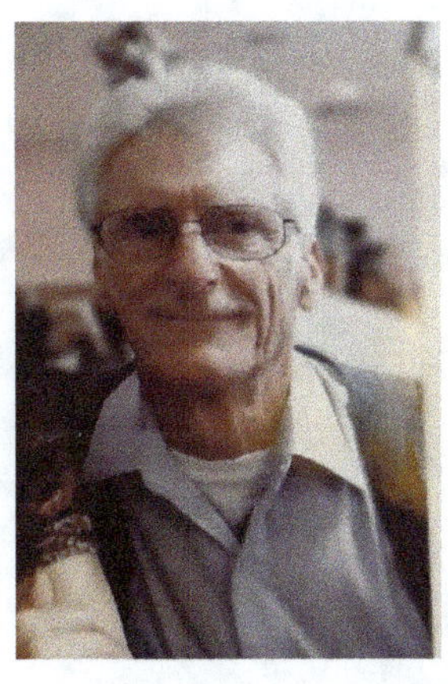

*Anthony R Balista 81, is a retired US Army Viet Nam Veteran with 6 overseas deployments of 2 each to Korea, Vietnam, and Germany in his career. Mr. Balista is also a retired Systems Engineer with a background in Communications-Electronics, Information Technology, Program and Engineering management, having managed large multimillion dollar defense industry programs.*

*He is a prolific technical writer, having written thousands of pages of technical manuals, test procedures, specifications and electronic communication standards, for the US Navy Trident Submarine, Center for Engineering and Systems Integration, The United States Army, Delphi Packard, ITT Corporation, RCA Corporation, and others.*

*He has four children and 9 grandchildren and currently resides in Warren, Ohio.*